TWILIGHT HUNTERS

WOLVES, COYOTES & FOXES

TWILIGHT HUNTERS

WOLVES, COYOTES & FOXES

Text by GARY TURBAK

Photographs by ALAN CAREY

 Northland Press

Contents

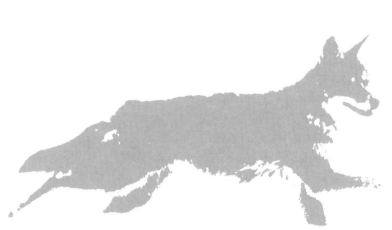

Cover photo: *Coyote in winter, Yellowstone National Park*
Frontispiece: *Gray wolf, Jasper National Park, Canada*

Text copyright © 1987 by Gary Turbak

Photographs copyright © 1987 by Alan Carey

All Rights Reserved

First Edition

Second Printing, 1988

ISBN 0-87358-453-8

Library of Congress Catalog Card Number 87-42821

Composed in the United States of America
Printed in Singapore through Palace Press

7.5M/11-88/0193

To Mom and Dad,
who taught me to love the wild world.

Red fox in winter, western Montana

Introduction

Of the thousands of animals with whom we share the planet, mankind is closest to the dog. Long before there were anthropologists and historians and biologists to record such things, mankind chose the dog as earthmate. Perhaps some cave-dwelling ancestor of yours and mine looked at the wild, howling curs around his camp and saw a shepherd for the flocks he would one day have. Perhaps he saw a sentinel to warn him of enemy approach. Perhaps he saw a confederate for the hunt. Or perhaps a friend for the ages.

But it could just as easily have been the animal that chose the man. Maybe it was the campfire's warmth that helped to tame the dog. Or, more likely, the steady supply of game that promised a full belly to any wolf that dared to dwell in the shadow of men.

We will never know for certain, of course, how or why the union of man and dog came to be. Suffice it to say that at some point in the daybreak of time, the two cast their lots together and have been housemates ever since.

But this book is about the dogs that did not come in from the cold. It is about that branch of the canine world that chose to remain free, chose to compete with, not befriend, mankind. It is about the wild dogs of North America—the wolves, coyotes, and foxes.

In the beginning was the wolf. At some point in the process we call evolution, doglike competitors disappeared, for one reason or another, from the scene. There remained one large carnivore that we, had we been there, would easily recognize as a wolf. From this seed—through the magic of natural selection, mutation, and survival of the fittest—have come the lesser wild dogs, the kin of the wolf.

Although all of these animals are members of the family Canidae (from which we get the common term "canine"), scientists have found among the wild dogs enough differences to split them into four genera. Although this book will refer to each species by its common name, it may be helpful to you to know how science sees them. Officially, they are:

Canis lupus . . . . GRAY OR TIMBER WOLF

Canis rufus . . . . RED WOLF

Canis latrans . . . . COYOTE

Vulpes vulpes . . . . RED FOX

Vulpes velox . . . . SWIFT FOX

Vulpes macrois . . . . KIT FOX

Urocyon cinereoargenteus . . . . GRAY FOX

Alopex lagopus . . . . ARCTIC FOX

By comparison, domestic dogs are classified as *Canis familiaris*. Different names notwithstanding, America's wild dogs share enough physical and behavioral traits so that even casual observers can recognize that they are cousins, if not brothers.

A number of characteristics help to distinguish the canines from other animals. Wolves, coyotes, and foxes have relatively long legs; four toes on each foot (with a fifth toe in the form of a dewclaw on the front feet); blunt, straight, nonretractile claws; an elongated skull; a long nose; a smooth tongue; and forty-two teeth, including

large and powerful canines. They sport a thick coat of hair and a long, bushy tail. There are scent glands on the feet and at the base of the tail near the anus. Their ears are pointed and stand erect. Most are shy and elusive. They produce one litter of young per year. They are also highly intelligent.

At the core of the canine's being is its ability to run. Wild dogs have been designed by evolution to move swiftly and with great endurance. Running as they do on their toes, canines are capable of quick turns, great speed, and sometimes almost unbelievable staying power. Dogs are the marathoners of the mammal world.

Locomotive capabilities have, in turn, helped determine what the canines eat and how they catch it. While the wild cats have developed a lifestyle based on stealth and the ability to stalk, canines thrive on speed and the open chase. Bears have largely given up their carnivorous way of life to exist on carrion and vegetable matter, which do not require pursuit. Canines, however, live by the chase and remain, for the most part, eaters of meat. Their teeth have become adapted for grasping and ripping, not chewing. Consequently, they gulp their food in large chunks and depend on a strong gastric system to break it down.

Long chases build up body heat, which must be dissipated. Pores, such as those humans have, would be of little use under all that fur, so canines have developed another, rather advanced, method.

Virtually all body cooling is accomplished by passing air over or through the tongue, mouth, and respiratory system. This is why dogs pant, and they may do so on a warm day even if they haven't been running. To ensure that the brain never overheats, warm blood headed from the heart to the brain is routed through a network of blood vessels that have just been cooled.

Wild dogs' sense of smell is keen, although some species have adapted to using other senses as primary hunting tools. Their keen noses are able to pick up minute traces of scent from the glands of other canines. Urine also carries odorous messages. It's believed a wild canine can, by sniffing a recent scent or urine deposit, not only tell which species has passed, but also know which individual it was and what mood the animal was in.

With a few exceptions (most notably, the wolf), wild canids are generalists and have adapted to a variety of climates, terrains, and food sources. Many of the small canines that typically hunt alone have learned to subsist on vegetable matter when meaty food becomes scarce. Coyotes and foxes, for example, are quite content to feast on melons and berries that would be of no interest to wolves, which must kill large prey that will feed an entire pack.

With relatively long legs designed for prolonged hunts and extended pursuit of prey, wild canines live in open country where running beats stalking for putting meat on the table. To some degree, the quintessential canine, the wolf, evolved in concert with the hooved animals it eats. The wolf's endurance forced the deer and antelope to become fast and wary. The ungulate's elusiveness forced the wolf into long chases and into packs. As biologist John McLoughlin has put it: "The wolf is father to the deer—which, in turn, is father to the wolf."

It's believed that caninelike animals first appeared in Earth's rich and diverse wild menagerie about 35,000 years ago. Wild dogs got along with people well enough until the latter discovered the science of animal husbandry, and the former learned that domestic prey were easier to catch than wild ones. From that day forward, the wolves, coyotes, and foxes of North America have been at odds with humans. Mankind's persecution has pushed some of them to the brink of extinction.

The pages that follow are meant to provide an up-to-date snapshot of each of these animals as it exists today. Some species you will probably never see. Others are familiar to all. And one or two you may know only as a piercing, hollow voice in the night. Remember that sound. And treasure it. It is as old as time, as wild as the wind, and as poetic as moonlight on snow. It is the trademark of the wolf and its kin.

Wolves

Oppressive cold follows the heavy snow to the northern woods. Falling like a great blanket over the forest and lakes, it turns everything brittle and seems to forbid sound. The air hangs clear and thin. Moonlight floods the forest. Then, from across the frozen lake, comes the first startling indication that there is life in this primeval iceland.

The howl begins low and melodious, rises to a piercing pitch, and seems to echo for a time after its maker has quit. The sound is lonely, eerie, haunting, surreal. A cry from the deep past. In a moment there is another. Then another. Soon the ridges resound with the chorus of a wolfpack on the prowl.

Shadows quaver, flow, and become wolves. Here one, there another, until eight of the beasts materialize in the moonlight. Together, they set off like apparitions across the frozen lake ice, the largest and strongest of them in front. For five miles they trot without pause. Then, as though they had run into an invisible wall, the wolves come to an abrupt halt and face stiffly into the woods at the edge of the lake.

The scent of a moose far upwind has reached their nostrils. The excitement among them becomes palpable as they wag their tails, lick each other's muzzle, and gather like soldiers around their leader general. When this commander wolf bounds into the woods toward the as yet unseen moose, the rest follow.

For a quarter mile they lurch through the deep snow. Then the forest gives way to a small clearing, and at the far side stand the moose—a cow and her calf. She sees the predators instantly, but does not move as the wolves bound silently across the meadow. When the predators close to within one hundred yards, the cow hazes her calf up to the trees at the edge of the clearing and turns to face the attackers. The wolves stop and appear uncertain about what they should do next.

Gray wolf howling, Canada

When two of the largest launch the final assault, the others follow, and the battle is fully joined.

With singular dedication, the predators pursue their common goal: to separate the calf from its mother. A frontal rush here, a rear attack there. Whirling at each assault, the cow sends one assailant after another into retreat. But the wolves are too many, and she can fend off only one or two at a time. Suddenly, several of the predators stand between her and the calf. Its eyes wide with fear, the young moose bolts and runs, and the wolves follow.

As the three-hundred-pound calf flees, two wolves leap at its rear, sinking their teeth again and again into the animal's rump. Two more run astride the calf, jumping and snapping at its throat. One finds a hold there and hangs on even as the young moose drags it twenty yards through the snow. Then, with the wolf still clamped to its throat, the calf stops running and stands for a moment in the ever-reddening snow. Another wolf sinks its teeth into the moose's nose. Three more attack its rear, and the calf goes down. For more than a minute its legs flail futily. Then all movement ceases. The wolves have won. In a moment, the rest of the pack arrives to join in the feast.

Instantly, the wolves set about devouring the fallen moose, ripping huge chunks of meat from the hindquarters and swallowing them whole. Strong jaws open the body cavity, and the heart, lungs, liver, and kidneys quickly disappear. So too

the tongue and nose. Gradually, the feeding frenzy subsides, the ripping and tearing of meat slows. Eventually, the wolves drift away from the carcass to rest atop a neaby ridge.

But digestion is a rapid process in a wolf stomach, and in a few hours each animal returns to gorge itself again. In the end, even many of the bones have been eaten, and all that remains of the moose is skull, large bones, hide, and hair. For a few more hours the wolves linger near the site of the kill. Then the pack leader gets to his feet, stretches, and trots off forty yards. Other wolves rise, but none follow. Returning, the leader nudges his underlings to their feet. Soon, there is a flurry of licking and tail wagging, and when the boss again heads off into the snow, the pack follows.

The Symbolic Wolf

Wolf! The very word strikes terror into many a person's heart, and it's unlikely that any animal has ever or will ever stir human emotions the way this creature does. The wolf is in our literature—from Aesop to Jack London to Little Red Riding Hood —and in our language—wolf whistles, human lone wolves, and wolfpacks of submarines. When we're in dire straits, the wolf is at the door, and when we eat in gulps, we're wolfing down our food. Hidden treachery is likened to a wolf hiding in sheep's clothing. Rightly or wrongly, the wolf has become a metaphor for cunning and bloodthirsty behavior.

But the animal in recent years has also become a symbol of free and unspoiled wilderness. Of a world yet untamed. Of starry landscapes where nature reigns supreme. Just as its eradication from most of the United States was a symbol of our human conquest over nature, its reemergence in the West (and potential reintroduction) symbolizes human commitment to the wild world.

People and wolves began as kindred creatures, both highly social beings that lived off the hunt and depended upon ritual to keep order. In the dark of prehistory, humankind made friends with the wolf and gave the animal a home in their camp. The two hunted together, and their spirits touched. But when people exchanged their hunting spears for shepherds' crooks, the two parted company. The wolf's predatory nature could not change, so they became enemies. Through history they have traveled, always at odds. Only recently has the cycle come full circle. Only of late has the wolf acquired human friends again.

Gray wolf, western Canada

The wolf's widespread reputation as a threat to humans is almost totally unfounded, and in the United States it has always been pure fiction. For about three years during the 1760s, wolves did terrorize human settlements in central France, reportedly killing ninety-three people, almost all of them children. This carnage was eventually blamed on a pair of animals thought to be dog-wolf hybrids. There is, however, not a single case of a wolf killing a human in North America. In fact, there is only one documented instance in which a non-rabid wolf even attacked a human on this continent, and even in that case, rabies may have been a factor.

Contrary to the belief of just about everyone, except the scientists who work with wolves, the animals are extremely shy around humans. Researchers have even been able to remove wolves from snares without tranquilizing them. Biologist David Mech once did so with an adult female simply by pinning her head to the ground with a stick (and, during part of the procedure, with only his gloved hand) while assistants put a collar on her and checked her teeth.

At one time, the gray wolf ranged throughout Canada and across almost all of the United States, including Alaska. Like most large predators, however, it suffered greatly at the hands of man. Today, Canada has perhaps 50,000 gray wolves, Alaska 10,000, and the rest of the United States

probably fewer than 1,300. In the lower forty-eight states, Minnesota has about 1,200, and Wisconsin and Michigan maybe a few dozen each. Recently, a handful of the animals have shown up in Montana.

The smaller red wolf is probably extinct in the wild, although there is a captive breeding population of the animals, and a program is underway to reintroduce them to their former range.

The wolf is the largest of the wild canines. Adult males average ninety-five to one hundred pounds and females about fifteen pounds less. The largest wolf ever weighed was an Alaskan animal that tipped the scale at 175 pounds. A big wolf might stretch six feet from nose to tail tip and stand three feet high at the shoulder. Its track measures four inches across.

As anyone who has ever been in wolf country or seen a western movie knows, the wolf's trademark is its howl—a musical, haunting, stirring sound born deep inside the animal's being. The wolf's howl, wrote Ernest T. Seton, "never fails to affect me personally with a peculiar prickling in the scalp that I doubt not is a racial inheritance from the Stone Age." The "chill-down-the-spine" reaction is not uncommon, but today more and more people regard the wolf's howl as a triumphant announcement that at least part of America is still truly wild.

Wolves howl to greet one another, to indicate

their location, to define their territorial boundaries, and to call together the pack. They may even howl just for the pure joy of it. Sometimes, a good howling session—accompanied by a lot of tail wagging and touching—precedes the hunt. Surprisingly, wolves will often answer a good human imitation of a wolf howl. They also make a variety of non-howling sounds not unlike those of domestic dogs.

In general, the gray wolf looks much like a large German shepherd, but its pelage ranges from pure white to coal black, with an almost infinite variety of grays and browns in between. Wolves in the Arctic are often white or nearly white, an adaptation to their snowy surroundings.

As a hunter, the wolf lives by its keen senses, particularly that of smell, which is said to be one hundred times more acute than that of humans. Wolf researcher David Mech once watched from an airplane as a pack of wolves caught the scent of a moose that was a mile and a half away.

Another wolf characteristic is its ability to cover great distances in search of game. Though it has been clocked at twenty-four to twenty-eight miles per hour, the wolf could not keep up that pace for very long. It can, however, trot at five miles per hour almost indefinitely and may spend as much as a third of its time on the move.

In the last century, when a lot of men spent a lot of time in pursuit of wolves, the animal's endurance grew to legend proportions. Author Stanley Young, collector of such accounts, tells of a female wolf in Arizona that happened to step into a trap attached by chain to a seven-pound piece of pipe. The wolf dragged the pipe a few hundred yards and lay down, but soon the trapper's hounds were put on its trail. With dogs and horsemen in hot pursuit, the wolf—still dragging its fetter—managed to stay ahead of its enemies for six grueling miles before a bullet ended its misery.

Another wolf, this time on Grand Island in Lake Superior, is reported to have led a dozen riflemen on a four-day chase before one of the men wounded the animal. For the next two weeks, the hunters trailed the wolf in shifts—sometimes even at night—until it was finally killed.

The Pack

The wolf's most indispensable personality trait is its ability to exist as part of a group, to form an attachment to others of its kind. Contrary to popular misconception, the wolf is generally a docile animal with a strong aversion to fighting. Though extremely strong and powerful, it settles disagreements with others of its kind through ritualized

battle, not combat. A glance or a growl is often all that's needed to determine dominance.

Wolves are social animals of the first order, and every group must have a leader. In the wolf pack, the literal top dog is called the alpha male, and all others are subservient to him. There is also an alpha female, to whom all other females are subordinate. Often, the top female also exhibits dominance over most or all of the pack males, with the exception of the alpha male.

An alpha animal looks like a leader — body erect, tail held out straight or arched high over the back, movements confident. By contrast, a lower ranking animal may sulk and cower, avoid eye contact with other wolves, and carry its tail low to the ground.

But the presence of leaders is just the first chapter in the complex book of wolf society. Each pack member occupies a definite rung on the social ladder, which makes it dominant to some members (unless it is the lowest) and subordinate to others (unless it is an alpha animal). When confronted by a more dominant wolf, the submissive one might roll on its back in a display of vulnerability, allow itself to be pinned to the ground, and even submit to having its muzzle chomped on

Gray wolves feeding on deer carcass,
Banff National Park, Canada

(without injury) by its dominant packmate. Imagine a dog cowering before an angry human master, and you have a fair picture of a submissive wolf deferring to one more dominant.

Submissive behavior plays a big role in maintaining peace within the pack, and all members except the alpha animals must display it from time to time. Naturally, the lower a wolf is in the hierarchy, the more practice it gets at being subservient.

In a large pack, the lowest wolves in the pecking order may become virtual "whipping boys," receiving attacks from and showing subservience to every other pack member. More importantly, they may also be the last to feed on a kill, and if there's not enough to go around, they must do without. In this way, the leaders can maintain their strength for hunting, thereby ensuring the continued existence of the pack.

If the gulf between the lowest wolf and the rest of the wolves becomes too great, the lowly one may actually be ousted from the pack. These animals sometimes become literal lone wolves, condemned to a life of avoiding all others of their kind. Unable to bring down large prey alone, they may be forced to exist on rodents and other small prey or to trail after a pack, gleaning meals from what is left behind. In a confrontation with a pack, the loner might be killed.

A new pack gets started when an individual leaves the group into which it was born, either because it is too independent to accept a subservient role or because it was driven out. If the lone wolf is lucky, it will find another of the opposite sex in the same situation, and the two will mate and produce a litter of pups.

The next year, the adults will breed again, but the yearlings, which have yet to reach sexual maturity, do not. The pack now consists of two adults, perhaps seven yearlings, and six new pups. The following year, some of the two-year-olds may leave to find new territory and start packs of their own. Those that remain will order themselves into an easily recognizable hierarchy with the original adults as the alpha male and female.

But the hierarchy is neither perfect nor permanent. A wolf may hold its position by virtue of especially close ties to the animal directly above it, and the pecking order within a pack changes as pups enter the group and as adults are affected by age, disease, and injury. Each wolf continually tests its position vis a vis its packmates, and when there is an opportunity to move up in the hierarchy, it does not hesitate to do so. Eventually, even the alpha animals must fall from their leadership positions.

One winter on Isle Royale in Lake Superior, researchers noticed that an alpha male had acquired a limp that grew progressively more debilitating. Bad weather severed the scientists' contact with the pack for a few days, and when the ani-

mals were again located, the alpha male lay dead. Examination of his remains indicated a severe case of arthritis, but the immediate cause of death was probably a leadership battle with another male wolf. Upon the demise of such a leader, the social hierarchy may come completely unraveled and a thorough shuffling take place.

Though the alpha male is the pack leader, he does not always rule with strict authority. Occasionally, traces of democracy show through as pack members essentially overrule a decision the leader has made about such things as which trail to take. Before starting off in a new direction or beginning a new activity, the pack often huddles around the leader, not unlike a football team around its quarterback. After much licking, sniffing, and tail wagging, the pack breaks huddle and takes off.

The presence of an understood hierarchy serves the crucial purpose of eliminating conflict. If animals as strong and potentially destructive as wolves had to fight continually to maintain their positions within the pack, injuries would be plentiful and hunting would suffer. Because pack members working together can bring down game that would elude an individual wolf, it is essential that they get along with each other. Each must know its place.

Unverified reports late in the last century spoke of fifty or one hundred wolves running together, but scientific wolf watchers say that a pack typically contains eight or ten members and that anything over a dozen is unusual (although packs with more than thirty members have been documented).

The size of a pack's territory varies greatly—from as small as fifty square miles to as large as 5,000 square miles (documented for one pack in Alaska). Usually, this domain remains the exclusive property of the resident wolves, with neighboring packs respecting the boundaries. Researchers have recorded instances in which a pack gave up chasing a mortally wounded deer after the doe crossed into another pack's territory. Two adjacent packs do, however, sometimes share a sort of "no wolf's land" that lies between the two more defined territories. Either pack may use this area, but neither does so very often.

Within its own territory, a pack makes regular rounds via a network of trails, roads, frozen lakes, ridgelines, and other travel routes. Some wolf runways remain in existence for many generations, and it was once erroneously thought that wolves always traveled in the same direction, (clockwise or counter clockwise, depending upon who was making the claim). Howling helps adjacent packs keep track of each other, and at dozens of prominent locations, resident wolves deposit urine and feces that identify their territory for other wolves.

The Hunt

The wolf pack exists, of course, to hunt. While wolves are not above feeding on bloated and rotting carrion, their attention is usually directed toward the largest herbivores available—moose, deer, and caribou. Where livestock and wolves come together, cattle and sheep also get put on the menu. Most often, wolves use their keen sense of smell to find prey, but they may also track a quarry through the snow. Because they are almost constantly on the move, they often simply stumble upon victims.

Contrary to popular belief, wolves cannot kill prey at will and do not normally kill more animals than they need to survive. If these misconceptions were true, the moose, deer, caribou, and other prey animals would have been wiped out long ago.

Under "normal" weather conditions, some sort of balance tends to exist between most predators and their prey. The predators typically cull the old, sick, and young, and populations of both species remain more or less constant. However, when weather or humans intervene to favor either predator or prey, nature becomes unbalanced, and populations can fluctuate wildly. Because there is seldom a "normal" winter in the North, wolves tend to exist on a boom and bust cycle.

Generally, more snow favors the wolf, while a dry winter gives the advantage to hooved prey. Still, in a good winter (good from the wolf's perspective, that is) the predators might kill only ten percent of the moose they encounter. In a winter with little snow, that figure may drop to two percent.

Much of what we know about the interaction of wolves and their prey emanates from work done by biologists Durwood Allen and David Mech on Isle Royale and in northern Minnesota. Their studies of the moose-wolf relationship on the Michigan island have added immeasurably to human understanding of both species.

Any ungulate attacked by wolves really has only two choices—to defend itself or to flee. Researchers report that healthy moose who choose to stand and fight survive much more often than those that run. The flailing hooves of an 800-pound moose (and the antlers, if it's a bull) make formidable weapons. Often, a moose will back itself up against a large tree to help protect its rear while it conducts a frontal defense. Wolves typically don't waste much time on healthy adult moose that stand their ground.

Durwood Allen speaks of the predator-prey relationship as one in which the wolves regularly give the moose a physical examination. If the moose passes the exam (that is, if it's found to be healthy), the wolves usually lose interest in it and race off to find another. In this way, the predators often end up killing the weakest moose available. But in a few weeks or months the wolves will return to test the healthy animal again.

A moose that runs, however, often finds itself in immediate trouble, as wolves simultaneously attack its rear, throat, and nose. David Mech once watched as a wolf clamped its jaws on the nose of a fleeing moose. Though the moose swung its head and lifted the wolf completely off the ground, the predator held on.

Once wolves commit themselves to a battle with a moose, the war of attrition may last for days. Some moose, of course, eventually escape, but others are slowly worn down by the ceaseless hit and run attacks. Finally, when the moose becomes too weak to remain on its feet, the war ends. Once a moose is toppled by the pack, it likely has but a few minutes to live.

An interesting sidelight to the moose-wolf saga concerns the unique defense that has evolved to protect each year's calf crop. Because newborn moose calves can neither run well nor defend themselves, they are extremely vulnerable to wolf attack. Consequently, the birth of calves has been synchronized so that all cows drop their young at approximately the same time. This floods the market with available prey, but it allows most of the

Gray wolf

young to gain some maturity while the wolves feast on the relatively few calves they can eat in a short time. If births were staggered, many more calves would be lost to the predators.

In some areas, deer have become the primary wolf prey. Unlike moose, a deer stands a better chance of surviving an encounter with wolves if it runs instead of fights. Because of its relatively small size, a deer is no match for a pack of hungry wolves, but with enough of a headstart, it can usually outrun its pursuers. The deer most often killed by wolves are those that for reasons of age, nutrition, or injury cannot make a speedy escape.

In the far North, caribou may be an important food source for wolves. Because these long-legged prey animals can outrun their pursuers on the open tundra, caribou-hunting wolves have learned to set ambushes, pursue fleeing caribou in relays, or simply chase a herd and wait for an animal to stumble.

A little more than a century ago, teeming bison herds formed a bottomless larder for wolves on the great North American prairie. There even evolved a separate subspecies of wolf that probably fed almost exclusively on bison meat. Buffalo wolves, the settlers called them. Larger and reportedly more aggressive than their woodland cousins, buffalo wolves frequently hunted in small groups of two, three, or four. After loping alongside a bison herd long enough to select a specific prey animal, the wolves attempted to cut their target,

usually a calf or young cow, from the herd. If they succeeded, it was just a matter of time until the lone bison fell to the wolf attack.

Newborn bison calves provided the wolves with a great bonanza, but the bison seemed to know that their size and numbers offered protection. Again and again, healthy adult bison formed a protective circle around vulnerable cows and their young, using their formidable horns and hooves to keep the predators at bay. For days at a time, the bison guard perimeter might keep the attackers away from the calves. If the circle remained tight and the defenders alert, the wolves would eventually have to look elsewhere for a meal.

One observer tells of seeing a ring of eight bison bulls protecting a single newborn calf from attacking wolves. In the distance grazed the main herd. Periodically, the bulls broke into a trot—still in tight formation with the calf at the center—and headed for the safety of the herd. But after one hundred yards or so, the calf would tire and lie down. The bison entourage would then stop and wait until the calf could once again travel. In this manner the bison escaped safely to the main herd.

The bison's trodding and pawing in a tightly formed defense sometimes left a circular scar upon the earth. Seeds from their shaggy coats fell here, and their droppings provided fertilizer. When vegetation returned to these blackened rings, it sometimes did so in a circle. Until about the 1960s there could still be seen on the prairies of the West vegetative remnants of the bison's great circular defense against the wolf.

But often enough the wolves, not the bison, prevailed. Artist George Catlin told of coming upon a bison bull alone on the prairie and surrounded by a pack of wolves: "We found that the bull had made great resistance, his eyes being eaten entirely out of his head, the gristle of his nose mostly gone, his tongue half eaten off, and the skin and flesh of his legs torn almost literally into strings." Round about, said Catlin, lay the bodies of several wolves that the bull had killed with its horns and hooves. In the end, the wolves won.

It is not uncommon for a pack to actually begin feeding on an animal while it is still alive. Observers report that some prey seem to enter a sort of tranquil state once escape becomes impossible. A fallen deer may raise its head and calmly watch the wolves that are ripping chunks of flesh from its hindquarters. Death quickly follows.

Because the availability of prey can be rather unpredictable, wolves have adapted to a feast and famine regime—gorging after a kill, then perhaps eating nothing for several days. It's therefore imperative that they make the most of every feeding opportunity by eating up to twenty pounds at a sitting. On average, a wild adult wolf might require five to ten pounds of meat per day, perhaps the equivalent of thirty deer per year.

The internal organs (except the intestinal tract) go first, then the fleshy parts of the carcass. Large pieces of meat are swallowed whole without chewing. In one wolf's stomach researchers found the liver, windpipe, tongue, one ear, both kidneys, and other assorted meat chunks from a recent caribou kill.

Temporarily satiated, the predators often wander off a short distance to rest. But wolf digestion is a rapid process, and in just a few hours pack members may begin drifting back to the kill for a second huge helping. Who knows when they may eat again? In this manner, a dozen wolves might polish off an entire moose in little more than a day. Usually, a pack will remain with a kill until everything edible has been eaten.

This often includes many of the bones, a food source to which the wolf's digestive system has neatly adapted. To prevent sharp slivers of bone from puncturing the intestinal tract, the wolf's system wraps indigestible pieces of bone in a protective coating of hair from the prey. The entire package is then passed in the feces.

Whenever wolves are on the move, they're hunting, and if there is prey in the area, it will be just a matter of time until the two come together.

Family Life

Like hunting, reproduction in a wolf pack also is something of a community affair. Normally, only one pair breeds in each pack, and the alpha male and female usually reserve breeding rights for themselves. But if either of the alpha animals does not show an interest in mating, that duty may be assumed by the beta (second-ranking) wolf of that sex. Occasionally, others in the pack may even produce litters. Later, most or all pack members will lend a hand with pup rearing.

On the surface, it might appear that restricting breeding rights to just one pair per pack is a rather inefficient way for a species to maintain itself. But an animal such as the wolf that has no natural enemies might soon reproduce beyond the carrying capacity of its habitat if all sexually mature animals bore litters. Also, annual mating battles between animals so potentially destructive could cause a lot of injuries.

Breeding season occurs in late winter, with the female giving birth to about seven pups (the range is five to fourteen) two months later. For the first few weeks, the youngsters are totally dependent on their mother's milk and protection and do not leave the underground den in which they were born. There is some evidence, however, that if the mother is killed before the pups are weaned, another female in the pack may begin to lactate and take over nursing duties.

At three or four weeks of age the youngsters are already engaging in the rough and tumble play that will help establish a dominance hierarchy among littermates. When the pups are about two months old, their parents may move them to what Durwood Allen calls "open-air kindergartens," places where they may be left above ground while the pack is off hunting. Sometimes, an adult "pup-sitter" may remain with the youngsters. Because of strong parental instincts within the pack, it's possible for pups to survive the death of both parents. By late summer or early fall the pups are big enough to accompany the pack on some hunting forays.

Before long, the pups are ready to begin eating the meat that will sustain them for the rest of their lives. The parents carry this new food to the den in their stomachs, then regurgitate it for the young to consume. Later, when the appetites of a growing litter overwhelm the food-gathering capabilities of the parents, other pack members join the meat brigade. A wolf observer in Colorado once discovered a den surrounded by 150 pounds of rotting meat that had been disgorged there for the benefit of pups. The wolves, however, had

Wolf pups, western Montana

abandoned the site, and the man suspected from the smell of the offal that he knew the reason why.

Sometime during their second or third year, the young become sexually mature. Interestingly, wolves and dogs crossbreed rather easily, and it's reportedly common in the North for Eskimos and Indians to intentionally inject wolf genes into their dogs' blood lines by tying female dogs in estrous out where male wolves may breed with them.

Wolf Hatred

Very few people—other than Eskimos and Indians—have ever had any use for—or love of—the wolf. The big predators were probably a problem from the very beginning for livestock-raising North American settlers. Puritan colonist Roger Williams called the animal "a fierce, bloodsucking persecutor." In 1630, the first bounty went on the wolf's head, and by the time the Civil War broke out, the animal had disappeared from most of the East.

In the vastness of the West it was different—at least for a time. While large numbers of bison still existed to fill wolf bellies, the settlers saw the predators as more of a nuisance than a threat. To be sure, inherited cultural hatred of the animal made it an enemy, but there was enough game for all. Pioneers shot plenty of wolves, but there was as yet no mandate to purge the prairie of the predators.

Wolves, in turn, were not particularly fearful of humans. After all, the sound of a rifleshot on the prairie was about as likely to be a call to dinner as a danger signal. A human hunter butchering a freshly killed bison might perform his work under the watchful eye of a gathering group of wolves. When he finished, he might be but a hundred yards distant before the scavengers moved in to strip the carcass clean.

But as the bison disappeared and the trickle of settlers became a flood, things changed. Seemingly overnight, cattle and sheep replaced the bison, and the wolf naturally turned its hungry attention to these new and vulnerable prey animals. In many places, wolves were blamed for the loss of a third of the annual calf and lamb crop.

And some ranchers claimed that the predators maimed as many cattle as they killed by repeatedly clamping their jaws on a cow's tail and pulling until the appendage was severed. Often, injuries were also inflicted upon the cow's hindquarters, and ranchers believed that bob-tailing, as the practice came to be called, was done by the wolves

Wolves jumping stream in Canada

largely for sport. Large numbers of bulls were also reported to have been emasculated by wolves.

It seemed that wolves were suddenly everywhere. "Frequently we count from three to eight wolves from the door of our ranch house in the daytime," wrote one Colorado stockman. "But they are most numerous and make their largest kills at night." Even conservation-minded Theodore Roosevelt referred to the wolf as "the beast of waste and desolation." The "nuisance" predator had become a significant economic threat, and the occasional skirmishes between man and wolf escalated into full-scale warfare.

Because shooting was much too slow and inefficient to make much of a dent in the wolf population, ranchers attacked with poison. Strychnine became as much a staple of ranch life as flour and coffee. Throughout much of the West there existed an unwritten agreement that no one should ride past the carcass of a dead cow, sheep, or bison without stopping to lace it with strychnine. One deadly bait station is reported to have reaped eighty-two wolves in twenty-four hours.

In the West and elsewhere, weapons in the wolf war were limited only by human imagination. Poison, traps, and rifles killed the most, but deadfalls and game pits were also used. Dens were

Gray wolf howling

dug up, flooded out, and dynamited. Wolves were captured, infected with mange, then released to infect others.

Hunting hounds were also employed—but not always successfully. One New Mexico rancher imported sixteen dogs that he hoped would reduce the local wolf population. The night before the first big hunt, he turned the dogs out of their pens so that they might get some exercise in preparation for the chase. Almost immediately, however, the dogs cut a fresh wolf trail and took off into the hills. Strung out in the pursuit, the dogs apparently happened one at a time upon a sizeable wolf pack. When the fight ended, only a single hound was left alive, but it was never able to hunt wolves again.

Perhaps the most ingenious method of wolf destruction was one employed by Indians and Eskimos in the far North. These hunters commonly took a long piece of sharpened whalebone, heated it to make it elastic, twisted it into a spiral or spring shape, then tied it in place. Once the bone had frozen, it could be untied and still hold its coiled shape. The harmless looking device was then coated with fat to attract the wolf and placed along a trail. Once inside the wolf's stomach, the bone would thaw and slowly straighten, puncture the animal's intestinal tract, and cause death.

Another northland technique was to freeze a knife in a block of ice with only the blade protruding. The blade was then coated with fat and the deadly device placed where a wolf would find it. In licking away the fat, the animal would cut its tongue, lick even harder at the smell of blood, and eventually bleed to death.

Through the latter part of the 1800s and into the 20th century the battle raged. Numerous state and local governments offered substantial bounties for dead wolves, and many stockmen's groups did the same. By 1914, the annual total of wolf bounties topped a million dollars.

One bounty hunter even employed his young son as a wolfer. When the man located a wolf den with pups, he sent his son headfirst into the burrow. Crawling along until he came to the animals, the boy grabbed one, then inched his way backward out of the hole. When he neared the den entrance, his father took hold of the youngster's legs and pulled boy and pup from the burrow. The process was repeated until the entire litter had been harvested.

Some skilled trappers made a good living killing wolves, but the bounty system, like most of its kind, did little to reduce the overall wolf population.

In 1915, under pressure from livestock interests, the federal government threw its vast resources into the war against wolves. The major livestock states were divided into eight predator control districts staffed with a virtual army of trappers and hunters. It was not long before the wolf population began an irreversible skid.

As more and more wolves were killed, some of those that remained took on a notoriety not unlike that of human outlaws of the same era. Here and there, an individual wolf would so impress the local human populace with its elusiveness that it would be talked about in almost reverent tones — and pursued without mercy. Often, it would be given a name: Old Three Toes, Whitey, the Winnipeg Wolf, and so on.

The Pryor Creek Wolf in Montana and the Sycan Wolf in Oregon specialized in slaying horses. The Aguila Wolf in Arizona was credited with killing sixty-five sheep in a single night. The Custer Wolf in South Dakota was blamed for $50,000 worth of lost livestock. Despite a $500 bounty put on its head by ranchers, the Custer Wolf ravaged 2,700 square miles from 1914 to 1920. Finally, the U. S. Biological Survey dispatched one of its best trappers to the scene, where he spent seven months working exclusively on capturing this one animal. In the end, of course, the man won.

Though cunning and strong, the wolf simply could not compete against this kind of persecution and federal funding. Rapidly, the midnight howl disappeared from the western air. Livestock deaths tapered off. Ranchers no longer saw wolves in daytime from their front doors. By the 1930s, the gray wolf had virtually vanished from the West.

The Wolf Today

Only in Alaska and around the Great Lakes has the wolf survived in the United States. Before Alaska became a state in 1959, wolves were bountied there, and they are still subject to sport hunting and trapping. Alaska game managers have used aerial wolf hunts to control populations they perceived to be a threat to moose and caribou. However, with almost limitless habitat (nearly eighty percent of the entire state) and a healthy population of 10,000 or so animals, the wolf in Alaska should be secure for some time to come.

The only other major U. S. wolf population is in northern Minnesota, where about 1,200 animals occupy an area approximately equal to five percent of the wolf's original range in the United States. And here in this wooded lake country dotted with farms, the wolf's last stand has become a political as well as a biological battle.

Since August 1974, when the Endangered Species Act went into effect, wolves have been completely protected in Minnesota. When the state wolf control program ground to a halt, farmers and deer hunters began complaining that the pred-

Gray wolf (black phase), Banff National Park, Canada

*Gray wolves moving through winter fog,
Jasper Park, Canada*

ator was wreaking havoc on livestock and game herds. The issue of state's rights versus federal control has also raised its head, and from time to time wolf politics heats up, the bumper stickers come out, and a wolf carcass or two gets thrown on the capitol steps.

The problem is this: While the wolf is endangered in the lower forty-eight states, it is fairly abundant in the northern third of Minnesota. Should Minnesota wolves therefore be treated as a species that is nearly extinct in the United States or as one that is rather plentiful and perhaps even a nuisance in one small area?

In 1978, the Minnesota wolf was reclassified from "endangered" to "threatened," which allows individual wolves to be killed if they cause problems. Protectionist groups have sued to prevent further degradation of the wolf's protective shield, but antiwolf sentiment still runs strong in some parts of the state, and it's estimated that poachers kill more than 200 wolves there each year.

Ironically, the wolf's strongest supporter, David Mech, believes that allowing hunters and trappers to kill a few of the animals each year might be good for the Minnesota wolf population. His reasoning is that this concession could help soften the hard core of wolf hatred while doing nothing to harm a healthy population of 1,200 wolves. The war of words—and sometimes bullets—continues.

The only other thriving U. S. wolf population outside of Alaska exists on the 210-square-mile Isle Royale in Lake Superior. Early in this century, moose apparently swam the fifteen miles from Canada to the island, found no threats from predators, and prospered. A few decades later, a pack of wolves established itself there, probably walking across the frozen lake from the mainland. Since then, the wolves and moose have undergone population fluctuations, but it appears they are both on Isle Royale to stay. Because the island is a national park, they are not likely to receive any human interference.

Although a few wolves still roam the woods of Wisconsin and Michigan, wolf watchers are not optimistic that they can continue to exist there for long. In 1974, biologists attempted to bolster Michigan's wolf population by releasing there four wolves captured in Minnesota. Within nine months, all four were dead—three from bullets and one from a collision with a car.

Other areas, including the Great Smoky Mountains and the Adirondacks, have been discussed as possible reintroduction locations for wolves. But when talk gets serious about transplanting wolves to new places in the United States, Yellowstone National Park usually heads the list. The last wolf was purged from the park in the 1930s, and wolf supporters believe it's time for the huge ecosystem to once again hear the howl of the pack.

Even the proposal of such a project, however, has become a sticky issue. The problem does not lie in the park, but rather in the rangeland that surrounds it. Having heard their grandfathers talk of the heyday of wolf predation on livestock decades ago, ranchers rightfully wonder about the wisdom of reintroducing the wolf where it might again prey on sheep and cattle.

Transplant proponents have proposed a series of concentric zones for the area—wolf protection in the center and livestock protection on the edges. But current law prohibits all killing of wolves in the West, and ranchers fear that they will have to become criminals by killing offending wolves or else sit helplessly by and watch their herds die. If it happens, the return of the wolf to Yellowstone will be as much a political accomplishment as a biological one.

Meanwhile, in northern Montana, the wolf has chosen not to wait. In 1985, a pack of perhaps a dozen wolves moved south out of Canada into Glacier National Park in northwest Montana. The following spring, this pack's breeding pair whelped a litter just north of the border, and in 1987 pups were born in Glacier Park. A few other wolves also have emigrated from Canada, and the U. S. wolf population in the northern Rockies now stands at about twenty animals. Wolf supporters are thrilled at this unexpected turn of events, but already there have been reports of livestock preda-

tion in the area, and it's possible that the Montana wolves could also become political hot potatoes.

Mexican Wolf

One other wolf, the Mexican, deserves mention here. As *Canis lupus baileyi,* the Mexican wolf is one of many gray wolf subspecies. Though possibly somewhat smaller on average than its more northerly cousins, the Mexican wolf is not ecologically or biologically different from the gray to any significant degree. Like so many other predators, it has captured the attention of researchers and other wildlife watchers because it teeters on the brink of extinction.

Originally, three gray wolf subspecies roamed the arid regions of Mexico. Because human presence (and, therefore, persecution) was rather limited, the animals survived fairly well there. For several decades earlier in this century, wolves from the Mexican pool of animals ventured north to replace those that had been trapped and poisoned in the United States.

Gray wolf, Canada

Beginning in the 1930s, however, Mexican ranchers adopted the same attitude toward wolves that their American counterparts had earlier developed. When cattle and other livestock came to the plateaus and highlands of north-central Mexico, the wolf suffered. Traps, poisons, and bullets killed wolves as efficiently in Mexico as they had in the United States, and it was not long before the predators were in serious trouble.

Two of the original three subspecies are already extinct, and scientists guess that the wild population of the remaining Mexican wolf may have dipped to as few as fifty animals. Though the wolves are protected by law in Mexico, some ranchers continue to kill them. Individual wolves may still make a rare appearance in Arizona, New Mexico, or Texas, but the few remaining animals seem for the most part to stay south of the border.

In 1982, Mexico and the United States approved a recovery plan that will attempt to reestablish the Mexican wolf on some of its former range. Between 1977 and 1980, four captured Mexican wolves were brought to the United States to form the nucleus of a captive breeding program. They have reproduced well, and there are now about thirty animals being held in four zoos.

Gray wolf, Banff National Park, Canada

Negotiations are currently underway to find a suitable location for the release of some of these wolves into the wild. A reintroduction such as this can be a long shot, however. To be successful, the release should involve a cohesive group of socially compatible animals that have not learned to associate humans with food. And, of course, a misguided rancher or wolf-hater could ruin the project by killing one or more of the animals. There is a possibility, though, that Mexican wolves may soon regain a bit of their former territory.

Red Wolf

The gray is not the only wolf in the United States. A smaller canine, the red wolf, clings to a tenuous existence and is perhaps already extinct in the wild. The red wolf once roamed from Florida to Texas and as far north as Indiana, but by 1970 its range had dwindled to just 1,700 square miles in Texas and Louisiana. Few, if any, wild red wolves remain, making the animal one of the most endangered mammals in the world and the wild canine closest to extinction.

The tawny, long-legged predator weighs between forty and eighty pounds and looks more like a gangly coyote than a gray wolf. In fact, the red wolf (which is usually more gray and black than red) holds something of a middle ground between coyotes and gray wolves. It is less pack-oriented than its gray cousin, yet more sociable than the coyote. Like the coyote, it has learned to live on small rodents and birds.

Persecution and habitat destruction by humans have hurried the red wolf toward extinction, but the coyote has played a major role as well. As wilderness became farmland and cities, the hardier coyote began to displace the less adaptable red wolf in many places. Once the coyote became established in these areas, the two began to interbreed, diluting the red wolf blood line. As coyotes and hybrids proliferated, the red wolf slipped closer and closer to extinction.

A two-pronged recovery plan now seeks to reverse that trend, but it may already be too late. Wildlife officials hope to establish a captive population of pure red wolves, then reintroduce the predator into former red wolf range. About seventy red wolves now live in zoos (most at the Point Defiance Zoo in Tacoma, Washington), and several more have been released in North Carolina as part of the first relocation project. There seems to be little hope, however, of ending the gene take-over by coyotes in the red wolf's current range. The only long-term solution appears to be the re-establishment of a wild wolf population from captive stock in areas that have no coyotes.

Coyotes

I will never forget the first time my wife saw a coyote up close and personal. She had drawn the antelope hunting permit that year, and I served as guide. Half a mile away that still morning on the Montana prairie, a coyote lingered on the hunt. We sat in the open next to a large rock, and I took from my pocket a magical little device called a predator call. Force a breath of air with proper intonations in one end, and a reasonable facsimile of a rabbit scream comes out the other. Often enough, it fills a coyote's head with images of an easy meal, and he approaches posthaste. I sent the rabbit over the airwaves, and the coyote came on the run, hell bent for the breakfast it had probably given up hope of finding.

When it had closed to within fifty yards, the predator took notice of the three rocklike forms sitting there where only one stone should be and began a circuitous fact-finding tour. Having no intention of shooting the animal, we sat and watched as it slowly circled us. In a few seconds, it arrived downwind of our position, caught our scent, and was gone.

About that time, three more coyotes—in a tight fighter pilot formation—burst over a knoll and bore down upon us. It seemed that the whole predatory world had spent the night in hunger. Shoulder to shoulder they ran. At twenty-five yards, we could see their bared teeth and darting eyes. Yet on they came. While I thrilled at having so wary an animal come so near, my wife's eyes flared wide with fear.

Deciding that discretion sometimes can be the better part of wildlife watching, I stood up. No animals, I think, have ever swapped ends faster than those three. In nanoseconds they changed from attacking killers into fleeing mongrels. Before I could so much as say "shoo," they were headed at top speed back from where they had come. The only creature for forty miles around more frightened than the coyotes was my wife. It took half an hour before she settled down enough to think about hunting antelope.

Coyote leaping, National Bison Range, western Montana

There is in this innocuous little incident something of a snapshot of the coyote—and the people who know it. In many ways, the Jeckle and Hyde characters we saw that morning on the plains are symbolic of the species as a whole. Incredibly brazen one moment, retreating the next. A marauding killer of sheep one night, a playful hunter of mice the next. It's sometimes difficult to believe that the shy coyote that sets up housekeeping deep in the Maine woods or on the vast expanse of a Nevada desert is even related to the one that prowls the streets of Los Angeles feeding on human garbage and cocker spaniels. But they are.

Equally dichotomous are the people who have opinions about the coyote. Just as my wife and I had strikingly different feelings about the approaching animals, so is public opinion split about the coyote in general. As a rule, farmers and ranchers hate them. So do many deer hunters who believe (usually mistakenly) that more coyotes mean fewer deer. So do some city residents who fear for the safety of their pets—and occasionally even their children.

Mark Twain once described the coyote this way:

[It] is a long, slim, sick and sorry-looking skeleton, with a grey wolfskin stretched over it, a tolerably bushy tail that forever sags down with a despairing expression of forsakenness and misery, a furtive and evil eye, and a long, sharp face, with a slightly lifted lip and exposed teeth. He has a general slinking expression all over. The coyote is a living, breathing allegory of Want. He is always hungry. He is always poor, out of luck and friendless. The meanest creatures despise him, and even the fleas would desert him for a velocipede. He is so spiritless and cowardly that even while his exposed teeth are pretending a threat, the rest of his face is apologizing for it.

But the coyote does have its admirers. Campers love to hear its howl in the twilight. Visitors to Yellowstone and other parks enjoy watching the predator ply its trade in the roadside grass. The animal is a ubiquitous symbol of the old West, wide open spaces, and success in the face of human persecution. Names like Coyote Creek, Coyote Meadows, and Coyote Peak dot maps of the West. The coyote is a tough little survivalist, and most people like a winner.

Adaptability

The key to the coyote's success lies in its ability to adapt to any situation, especially the presence of humans. The large predators that lacked this skill soon found themselves retreating before the rush of human settlement. The grizzly and wolf have all but disappeared from the United States, and the cougar has sequestered itself in the forested wilds of the West. But the coyote, which saw humankind as nothing more than an annoyance (and often as a meal ticket), quickly learned to live among the human tide.

In her book *God's Dog,* naturalist Hope Ryden describes the coyote's versatility this way: "The adaptable coyote is not only capable of bivouacking where he pleases, he seems able to adopt any number of lifestyles. He can hunt either by day or by night, dine on fresh meat or survive off carrion, raid town garbage pits or feast on wild fruits and berries, den in burrows or whelp in conduit pipes, run in packs or operate as a loner."

With a range that extends from Florida to Washington and from Costa Rica to Alaska, the coyote is one of the most successful mammals in the Americas. It is found in every state except Hawaii and in most Canadian provinces. No one has counted them, of course, but they certainly must number in the tens of millions.

This was not always so. When Europeans first set foot on North American soil, there were perhaps only a few million coyotes, their range limited to what are now the western states. Native Americans had domesticated some of the animals and had invited the coyote into their mythology as a conniving, unscrupulous opportunist that never-

theless merited respect because it always got what it wanted.

The coyote's scientific name, *Canis latrans,* means "barking dog," but settlers often referred to the predator as a brush wolf or prairie wolf. The word "coyote" is an adaptation of "coyotl," the name that Spanish explorers once heard Indians use. Incidentally, both pronunciations—ˈkī-ōt and kī-ˈōt-ē—are correct.

As European settlement spread west across the continent, coyotes moved east. Where traps and rifle balls eliminated the wolf, the coyote moved in to take its place. When pack trains headed north to the Alaskan gold fields, coyotes followed to feed on the horses and mules that died along the way. Midway through the last century, the coyote crossed the Mississippi and began working its way east. In the 1920s and '30s it arrived in New England and other areas along the Atlantic Coast.

With nineteen recognized subspecies, the coyote is really many animals. Most of these, however, are distinguished by subtle changes in dentition or skull size that are of little concern to anyone except scientists. Coyotes do, however, vary significantly in size and color from one part of their range to the next. Experts believe that crossbreeding between coyotes, wolves (red wolves, most likely), and dogs is responsible for many of the differences.

Though size varies greatly with geography and diet, a typical male coyote might stand twenty inches tall at the shoulder, measure four feet from nose to tail tip, and weigh thirty pounds. A few individuals have tipped the scales at nearly fifty pounds, and females are usually somewhat smaller. The coyote's fur is long and soft and comes in endlessly mottled shades of gray and brown, although individuals can range from nearly jet black to nearly pure white. Long legs propel the predator to about thirty mph, although bursts topping forty mph have been reported.

Scavenger and Hunter

Like most predators, coyotes have keen senses. A few years ago, researchers at Colorado State University set out to discover whether coyote hearing, smell, or sight was primarily responsible for its skill as a predator. In a series of experiments in a closed room, they exposed coyotes to rabbits under a variety of sensorial situations. Attacks on munching, rustling rabbits were compared with those against quiet prey. All light was removed to see how the coyote fared in complete darkness.

Odors were pumped into the room to mask the prey's smell. When all the data were in, the scientists concluded that hunting coyotes rely primarily on vision, but that smell and hearing also play important roles. This seemed logical, the researchers said, for a predator that evolved on the short-grass plains where large prey could often be seen before it was smelled or heard.

If there is, however, one part of the coyote's anatomy that can take credit for its success, it is the stomach. It has been said that the coyote's favorite food is anything the animal can chew; it doesn't have to be digestible. Harness buckles, shoe leather, and chunks of tires have all been found in coyote stomachs. So have lizards, snakes, crickets, and meat from every creature from grizzly to skunk. And, of course, some deer and more than a few sheep end up on the coyote dinner table.

Coyotes—like men, bears, and pigs—are omnivores. When given the opportunity, they don't hesitate to raid orchards and strip apples, pears, peaches, and a host of berries from trees. Their favorite vegetable food appears to be melons, and some coyotes have become experts at selecting only the best fruit. Melon-munching coyotes have

Coyote

virtually destroyed some farmers' crops by taking just one bite from each of hundreds of ripe melons.

More commonly, coyotes subsist on deer and elk carrion in the winter and a variety of mice and other small rodents in the warm months. On a typical hunt, a coyote trots across a grassy meadow, listening for the squeak or rustling of a mouse. When it comes, the predator may freeze like a setter on point, its ears cocked for another indication of exactly where lunch might be hiding. When it has slunk within a few feet of its prey, the coyote rears up on its hind legs and pounces on the rodent with its front feet. In its enthusiasm, a rodent-bound coyote may end its leap on its nose or somersault to a landing.

A quick bite to the head dispatches the rodent, and the coyote swallows it whole. It's estimated that coyotes catch between ten percent and fifty percent of the rodents they stalk. More than thirty undigested mice have been found in the stomach of a single coyote, indicating a very busy hunter indeed. One researcher has calculated that an adult coyote needs about one and a half pounds of meat per day, much less than most people (especially sheep ranchers) would guess.

A coyote leaps through the snow in western Montana

Getting at mice beneath a crust of snow can be difficult, which often makes winter a hungry time for coyotes. Occasionally, a coyote substantiates its reputation for cleverness by employing an elk or bison as an assistant. As the ungulate uses its large hooves and snout to sweep snow away from the grass it wants, mice are routed from their sanctuaries. More than one coyote has been seen hovering near a feeding elk or bison, waiting for a chance to rush in—even under the belly of a bull—and catch a mouse as it flees.

Larger prey include ground squirrels, marmots, prairie dogs, and rabbits. Though coyotes are often blamed for locally low deer numbers, their infrequent predation probably has little or no effect on deer populations. When coyotes do prey on adult deer, they kill the weak, lame, sick, and old. Under normal circumstances, a healthy buck or doe is more than a match for coyotes. Coyotes have, however, been known to decimate local antelope fawn populations and to kill deer fawns as well. Usually, however, does are able to protect their young from the coyotes.

Montana biologists Kenneth Hamlin and Larry Schweitzer once had a rare look at exactly how deer fawns might fall prey to coyotes. From a low-flying small plane they spotted a mule deer doe with newborn twin fawns atop a ridge. A pair of coyotes was hunting nearby, and it wasn't long before the predators spotted the potential prey.

While one coyote remained forty yards from the deer, the other circled out of sight to a spot on the far side of the animals. The first coyote then made a frontal attack, and the doe chased it about ten yards before returning to her fawns. When the coyote rushed again, the doe pursued the predator for about one hundred yards before returning to her young. But she was too late. The second coyote had already dragged one of the fawns into a juniper bush. Moments later, it died.

The coyotes don't always win, however. In the 1940s, Charles Vest of the Wyoming Game and Fish Commission chanced to observe a remarkable drama. One day in the wilds of Wyoming, Vest looked up to see a buck deer in hot pursuit of a large male coyote. Eventually, the deer overtook the coyote, knocked it off its feet, and began to pummel the predator with its hooves. After receiving a thorough beating, the coyote crawled into a brush patch, but the deer, not yet satisfied, began to circle menacingly. When Vest approached and frightened the buck off, he found the coyote badly trampled and put it out of its misery.

Though elk are too large to have anything to fear from coyotes, many of them do end up on the coyote dinner table. Winter can be hard on elk, and spring often reveals meadows dotted with the carcasses of elk that perished in the cold. This, of course, provides easy pickings for hungry coyotes.

In her book, Hope Ryden describes one such poignant incident: A huge bull elk had walked into a streambed and had become mired in the mud. Weak from a winter with little food, it could not extricate itself. When Ryden happened upon the scene, an eagle perched on the elk's antlers, waiting. Eventually, the old bull became too weary to hold its head above the water, and the struggle ceased. Soon, coyotes began arriving from all directions. Over the next few days, several of the scavengers made the long leap from the streambank to the elk's back. One pair claimed control of the carrion, allowing some fellow coyotes to feed, but chasing others off. In short order, virtually all available meat had been stripped from the carcass.

Cooperation

Unlike wolves, coyotes do not usually hunt in packs. In summer and early fall, a family unit may hunt together as the pups learn the predator trade, but coyotes usually work alone or in pairs. Coop-

Two coyote pups looking out of den, western Montana

erative hunting between two coyotes appears to occur fairly often. Because coyotes often mate for life, two hunters on the prowl may well be a mated pair. The two may travel together for a distance, split up briefly as each checks likely looking cover for prey or carrion, then resume a side-by-side journey. Large catches probably are shared.

But sometimes, as with the Montana deer kill mentioned earlier, cooperation goes far beyond traveling together. Naturalist George Bird Grinnell once witnessed an impressive display of coyote teamwork. From atop a small butte, he saw a doe antelope being pursued by a coyote. The tongues of both animals dropped from their mouths in fatigue as they loped across the plains, and Grinnell guessed that they had already run a great distance. "Suddenly," he later wrote, "almost at the heels of the antelope, appeared a second coyote, which now took up the running, while the one that had been chasing her stopped and sat down." Into the distance the pair ran, but the antelope bore steadily to its left, in effect traveling in a large circle. Watching all this, the resting coyote trotted off 200 yards to where it appeared the antelope might next pass. There the refreshed predator hid in the grass.

Coyote at dusk, Yellowstone National Park

As Grinnell watched the weary antelope approach, he could see two coyotes in pursuit, one quite close and the other farther back. It appeared that the closest one had recently picked up the chase and that the distant coyote was the one that had first lain in ambush near the butte. As the antelope neared the hidden coyote, the predator repeatedly peeked above the grass to gauge the pronghorn's precise route, then crawled on its belly so that it might lie directly in the doe's path. "When the antelope reached the place where the coyote lay hidden, he sprang up and in a jump or two caught her neck and threw her down," wrote Grinnell. In a moment, the other coyotes arrived to join in the feast.

Though it probably doesn't happen very often, some observers have been privileged to see a much more sophisticated form of coyote cooperation. M. P. Skinner, a well-known naturalist early in this century, saw the following incident unfold on the shore of Yellowstone Lake.

A small flock of pelicans was fishing in the shallow water near shore when two coyotes emerged from the nearby woods and stalked as close to the water's edge as they could without being seen. It was obvious to Skinner—and apparently to the coyotes—that there was no way for the predators to get to the birds without alarming them.

Suddenly, one of the coyotes raised its tail above its hiding place and began moving it slowly

back and forth. Apparently curious, the pelicans began wading ashore to investigate. They were, however, too wary to come all the way out of the water. After a few minutes, the tail-waving coyote strode out onto the beach in full view of the birds. The other coyote remained hidden. The exposed coyote raced up and down the beach, ignoring the pelicans but making great show of tossing pieces of wood into the air, chasing its tail, and in other ways being totally conspicuous. Then it trotted off away from the birds.

Still curious—and perhaps remembering the odd waving tail they had seen earlier—the pelicans marched ashore and hesitatingly approached the spot from which the coyote had emerged. The hidden coyote then burst from concealment and grabbed one of the birds. The last Skinner saw of the predator, it was headed with its catch in the direction the first coyote had taken.

Another type of cooperation involves a symbiotic relationship with another predator. Though they would at first glance seem to be unlikely partners, coyotes apparently team up fairly regularly with badgers to capture burrowing prey. Typically, it seems to work this way: A coyote and a badger travel together across the prairie, the

Coyote feeding on elk carcass, National Elk Refuge, Wyoming

coyote probably stopping often to let the short-legged badger catch up. If the coyote can catch a meal with its speed and quickness, the two may share the feast (although it's just as likely that the coyote will dissolve the partnership at that point).

However, a prey animal that lives underground—a prairie dog, for example—usually can escape a coyote attack simply by diving into its burrow. When this happens, the badger takes over. With its sharp claws and powerful forequarters, the stout badger begins to enlarge the burrow and pursue the prairie dog into its underground haven. The coyote, perhaps anticipating where the burrow's back door may be, assumes an alert position a few feet away.

At some point in the excavation, the prairie dog may panic and burst from the tunnel's second entrance. If the coyote has guessed right, it is close enough to overtake the rodent before it can disappear into a neighboring burrow. Again, the two predators may share the catch, although the coyote could easily run off with a small rodent if it chose to do so. Since the badger does most of the work and does not always share in the spoils, it appears that the partnership is of greater benefit to the coyote.

Coyote howls on a bleak January afternoon, western Montana

Earning a Reputation

Another frequently cited hunting scenario supposedly takes place this way: The coyote finds a conspicuous spot—perhaps a knoll or game trail—and lies down on its side. There it lies motionless for whatever minutes or hours it may take to attract the attention of a raven, crow, or magpie. Eventually, the sight of a supposedly dead animal lures one or more of the birds in for a closer look, at which point the coyote leaps up and makes a meal of the scavenger.

Though stories about the coyote's hunting prowess do at times seem to defy belief, there certainly is more than a little truth in some of them. "Roadrunner" cartoons notwithstanding, the coyote is generally recognized as a clever, determined, wary predator and scavenger that almost always finds a way to get what it wants while avoiding capture.

Trappers have long found the coyote to be a worthy opponent. If ever a coyote escapes from a trap, it is almost certain never to get caught again, and more than a few trappers have told of coyotes that seemed to haunt their traplines, repeatedly and intentionally springing traps without getting caught.

Wyoming trapper Oren Robinson once watched as a trapped coyote pulled the trap loose from its moorings and started off slowly across the prairie. Attached to the chain was a three-pronged grappling hook designed to prevent an animal from getting very far.

And it was working. Every few steps, the hook would catch on a rock or sagebrush and halt the coyote's escape. With jerking and tugging, the coyote would pull the hook free, only to get hung up again a few seconds later. Finally, Robinson reported, the coyote walked back to the hook, picked it up in its mouth, and traveled some distance unfettered. However, when the coyote jerked itself to a halt by stepping on the chain, it seemed to become confused and gave up the escape attempt.

Though legends did not grow up around the coyote the way they did about the wolf, many communities in the West had a coyote or two that everyone knew by reputation if not by sight. In his book *The Clever Coyote,* naturalist Stanley Young records the exploits of a particular Caddo County, Oklahoma, coyote. "Old Three Toes and his co-killers were a hard-boiled lot, whelped in a region where the length of a coyote's life depended a good deal upon the length of his legs and on the same dimension in his head," wrote Young. "They belong to a superior breed, developed by the very

Young coyote, western Montana

methods that had been designed for their undoing, and Old Three Toes was the strongest, fleetest, wisest of the clan."

With one toe missing from his right front foot, Old Three Toes left his footprint calling card wherever he chanced to step in the soft Oklahoma mud. For six years, he and others of his kind wreaked havoc on the sheep herds around the community of Lookeba. Local men caught plenty of coyotes in their traps, but never Old Three Toes, although his missing digit suggested that once—perhaps in his youth—he might have been briefly detained by a trap.

Expensive hunting dogs were brought in to do what the traps could not. The hounds ran down a lot of coyotes, eliminating the slow, the unwary, and the young, but Old Three Toes was not among them. Over a period of time, the number of coyotes decreased dramatically, but livestock predation did not. Fewer tracks were being found, but these invariably indicated that only the largest of the coyotes were left. People began to fear that their persecution had somehow caused the predators to evolve into a sort of super coyote. There were even rumors that Old Three Toes and his cohort might be wolves, not coyotes.

Eventually, a government hunter arrived. In a month of trapping and shooting, he killed nineteen of the largest, toughest, rangiest coyotes that remained. It seemed that only the coyote with the missing toe was left. Then one morning the hunter found Old Three Toes in a trap. Though not a wolf, it did weigh forty-five pounds, almost twice that of some lesser coyotes. For days, farmers and ranchers made brief pilgrimages to where the coyote corpse lay. The reign of predation that had cost them more than $10,000 was over, but a living legend had died too.

Besides earning a reputation as a killer of sheep and other livestock, the coyote has also impressed mankind with its ingenuity. Called "crafty" or "wiley" by virtually every author to write about it, the coyote has acquired a mystique that sometimes looms much larger than the animal itself. Were the coyote big enough to occasionally attack a human, it almost certainly would have moved ahead of the wolf, cougar, and grizzly in the list of the most hated animals on the American frontier.

But its cleverness did not escape notice. In *The Voice of the Coyote,* author Frank Dobie records an incident told to him by a man who claimed to have witnessed it while hunting in Mexico: On an overcast day that threatened rain, the man saw a coyote approach a prairie dog colony. The predator made a dash for a prairie dog or two, but as usual, the rodents escaped into their burrows. The coyote, however, did not leave. Instead, it began digging furiously at the mounds surrounding the entrances to three adjacent prairie dog burrows.

At first, the hunter thought the coyote to be a rather stupid animal, as it could never hope to dig a prairie dog out of its underground sanctuary. But about the time the rain started to fall, the man began to see method in the coyote's madness. The purpose of its digging had been to tear down the mound that surrounded the burrow entrance. This dirt the coyote fashioned into a large "V," with the open end pointing uphill and a burrow entrance at the apex. The predator engineered a repetition of this process at two more holes, then hid itself in the grass near one of the entrances.

The rain came in pelting sheets, pouring down the slope in hundreds of rushing rivulets. With the entrance mounds removed and the coyote's makeshift dikes in place, some of these little streams ran directly into the burrows. As the storm raged, the coyote remained at its post. When enough water had cascaded into the burrow, a wet prairie dog came up for air and was immediately snatched by the waiting coyote.

A Texas cowhand, J. W. Maltsberger, told Dobie of another way in which the coyote uses its wits to outmaneuver prairie dogs. Prairie dogs typically emerge from a night's rest an hour or so after dawn. One day at first light, Maltsberger observed a coyote busily stopping up prairie dog burrows with dirt. It plugged a few adjacent holes, then moved off a fair distance and waited. Before long, prairie dogs began emerging around the colony. Still, the coyote waited. Soon, however, one of the rodents grazed its way into the area where the coyote had done its work. In a flash, the coyote bore down on the prairie dog, which ran immediately to a mound where yesterday there had been a burrow. Finding no avenue of escape, it turned to flee in another direction, but the coyote was already upon it.

Getting to Know Ewe

If prairie dogs, mice, and an occasional antelope fawn were all that coyotes killed, humans might treasure them the way they do deer and songbirds. But coyotes long ago learned that farms and ranches mean livestock and that calves, pigs, and sheep are easy to kill and exceedingly good to eat.

In fairness to the coyote, however, it must be pointed out that very few calves die at its jaws. In most cases, a cow is more than capable of defending her calf from coyotes, and many cattle ranchers harbor no ill feelings toward the coyote. In some places, coyotes do kill a fair number of pigs, but usually swine are housed and cared for very near the farmer's house and other buildings, and this tends to discourage coyote attacks. Also, the coyote that takes on a 300-pound hog is going to have a tough job arranging for dinner.

Persecution

It was the coyote's taste for mutton that long ago marked the predator for persecution. In 1804, Lewis and Clark provided the first good description of the doglike animal that inhabited the western plains. In 1823, zoologist Thomas Say gave the animal a name, and in 1825 the state of Missouri became the first of many to put a price on the coyote's head. Settlers in the West shot coyotes on sight, and the federal government sent small armies of trappers and hunters into the field to do battle with the predator.

As with most such schemes, the coyote bounty system was a colossal failure. Not about to kill the goose with golden eggs, some trappers routinely released females so that they might produce yet more coyotes. Many a bounty was collected for the scalp of a farmyard dog that had chanced to die. Coyote skins tended to migrate toward the state or county paying the highest bounty, and many hides were bountied more than once, especially after they had become a bit ripe, discouraging close inspection by government clerks.

In places where pups brought a lower bounty than adults, some enterprising individuals took to coyote ranching. In the spring they would venture afield with shovel in hand to dig the young pups from their dens. Throughout the summer the captives were kept in fenced enclosures and fed horsemeat. By fall, the value of the now fully grown young had increased considerably, and they were harvested and bountied.

In the 1930s, after the federal government authorized a sweeping control program to reduce coyote numbers, the skirmish lines melded into a war. The belief that "the only good predator is a dead predator" permeated all levels of government and agriculture, and a plethora of poisons flooded the land. Across the West, ranchers and professional government trappers set out baits of horsemeat laced with arsenic, cyanide, strychnine, or thallium sulfate.

One of the best tools for killing coyotes is a device called the "coyote getter." A tube driven into the ground houses a small explosive charge or spring and a bite-sized portion of sodium cyanide. The device is planted so that the upper end, where the trigger lies, is about at ground level. The affair is topped off with a piece of wool or rabbit fur doused with a scent appealing to coyotes. When one of the predators catches a whiff of the lure, it investigates and—in typical coyote manner—tugs on the scented bait. This detonates the explosive

Coyote with mallard, western Montana

or trips the spring, which propels the charge of poison into the coyote's mouth.

A skilled trapper might be able to knock off a dozen coyotes a day with coyote getters, and one federal trapper reported killing 522 in a single month. Crude and cruel as it might be, the device was a relatively safe method of eliminating coyotes, as it did not often kill other species. The problem—as far as ranchers were concerned—was that it killed only one coyote at a time. After each detonation, the device had to be reset.

In the 1950s, a more efficient killer came along. Compound 1080 (named for the invoice number of the substance) is a white, saltlike powder that is essentially odorless and tasteless. Highly soluble in water and easily absorbed through an animal's gastrointestinal tract, 1080 seemed the perfect poison. And because 1080 is more lethal to canids than to other species, it was touted as the perfect poison for ridding the West of the coyote scourge.

Half an ounce of 1080 injected into a 1,000-pound horse carcass could theoretically kill more than 11,000 coyotes. And because it broke down very slowly, 1080 kept on working long after the bait had been set. A chunk of treated meat dumped on the prairie could remain potent for months in cold weather.

Whole steer and horse carcasses were impregnated with 1080 and left at prominent places on the high plains to work their lethal magic. Several hundred thousand coyotes died, but so did tens of thousands of other animals—bobcats, foxes, domestic dogs, eagles, and virtually every other creature with an appetite for meat (including the kit fox and the red wolf, two species now on the brink of extinction). Compound 1080 remains lethal even in the body of its dead victim. A coyote or other consumer of 1080 may be fed upon by any number of scavengers, each of which may pass the poison on to yet another series of victims.

Rescue from this pervasive poison rode in on the shoulders of the environmental movement in the 1960s. In a relatively short time, predators came to be seen as valuable components of a healthy ecosystem, not as vermin to be exterminated. There arose a hue and cry against indiscriminate killing and nonselective poisons (especially those like 1080 that were responsible for the deaths of numerous bald eagles). In 1972, the Environmental Protection Agency banned the use of 1080, but that prohibition has recently been lifted for some uses of the poison.

Ranchers have tried a variety of other techniques to prevent coyotes from killing sheep. Some report reduced predation when guard dogs (several different breeds have been tried) are allowed to run with the sheep. Guard mules—and even guard llamas—have also been employed, usually with less than great success. Bait stations laced with birth control chemicals were largely abandoned when too few coyotes ate the adulterated meat.

Some ranchers tried hanging special collars on the necks of their sheep. Acting on the belief (usually correct) that just a few coyotes do most of the killing, they hoped to kill or repel only the offenders. Some collars contained odors thought to be repulsive to coyotes, such as essence of skunk or cougar urine. Other collars held poisons that were intended to kill the predators when they bit the sheep on the neck. The devices eliminated some coyotes, but often the survivors simply learned to avoid sheep with collars.

One innovation that has been beneficial to coyotes is the change that has taken place in the public attitude toward predators. Most people today know that predators play an important role in the wild world. Gone are the days when an animal could be considered inherently evil and an attack made on its very existence. To be sure, some ranchers (often with justification) still plead for a reduction in coyote numbers, and several million dollars are still spent each year on predator control. But the all-out war against the coyote is over. And the coyote has won.

The Victorious Coyote

For every new human weapon aimed at its destruction, the coyote has countered with a behavioral change that produced more coyotes or

slowed the kill rate. A coyote that escaped from a trap might thereafter make an avocation of setting off traps. It might also teach its young to avoid the steel devices. In general, coyotes became more wary, stayed away from humans, and conducted more of their business at night.

As the weak, stupid, and unwary were eliminated, there did seem to evolve a sort of super coyote, one quite capable of dealing with its human enemy. One biologist has written: "We, with our persecution of the coyote, have added another parameter to natural selection, with the result that coyotes are now larger, smarter, more adaptable, faster, and more cunning than when white men first entered the coyote's territory."

They're also more numerous. One estimate is that the United States was home to perhaps two to three million coyotes when the first Europeans set foot on American soil. Today, after a century and a half of shooting, trapping, and poisoning, there are many times that number. The more that were killed, the more there were. It was as if the coyote were playing a cruel biological joke on its tormenters.

One adaptation that helped the coyote deal with persecution is something called density dependent reproduction. It works this way: When a coyote population is at a "normal" level, a certain percentage of females breed and produce "average-sized" litters. Though the coyotes don't know it, their goal is to maintain the status quo.

But if the number of local coyotes plummets, some inner trigger is tripped, and the remaining

animals work feverishly to replace the lost colleagues. More females begin breeding, and the litters get larger. In documented cases, a sharp decline in coyote numbers caused the proportion of breeding females to skyrocket from thirty-two percent to ninety percent, and the average litter size to increase from three or four to eight or nine. Quite literally, the killing of coyotes in a given area can serve to increase, not decrease, the coyote population.

Persecution also helped push the coyote into virtually every corner of potential habitat. When repeatedly disturbed by men or dogs, a coyote may forsake its home range for a more trouble-free area. About the time the war on coyotes was raging wildly, the predators were busy expanding their range into areas of the East where they had never before existed. In the 1920s and 1930s, the howl of the coyote came to grace the night air in places like New York, Vermont, and Florida.

In recent years, coyotes have become rather controversial in Maine and a few other states, primarily for their supposed decimation of the deer population. They do not, of course, pose any great threat to deer, but try telling that to a hunter who has seen little game.

A coyote rests near its den

Actually, the coyote that recently emerged in New England may well be part wolf. The theory is that as the coyote migrated eastward from the plains, it interbred with wolves in Canada, sending its hybrid offspring on to populate the northeastern states.

Unlike most wild creatures, coyotes are able to mate with other species and produce fertile progeny. Wolves are the most likely interspecific partners, but the larger predators are often more inclined to eat a coyote than to mate with it. In fact, the natural hostility between the two species is probably the only reason that the two animals did not long ago interbreed themselves into a single species. Still, wolf-coyote unions do sometimes occur (usually with the smaller and now almost extinct red wolf).

Coyotes also have been known to mate with a variety of domestic dog breeds, producing a sometimes strange array of progeny. The farmyard mongrel may be the coyote's worst enemy most of the year, but come breeding season there often exists a truce between coyotes and dogs of the opposite sex.

Were it not for a quirk in the genetic transfer, the offspring of these unions might threaten to irreparably dilute the wild coyote strain. If, for example, every half-breed were to mate again with a pure coyote, it would not be long before some local populations would be neither dog nor coyote but rather some mixture thereof. When the hybrids reach breeding age, however, they display the random estrous cycle of domestic dogs that can come into heat at any time of the year. Coyotes, on the other hand, maintain a precise annual schedule that has them breeding only during mid-winter. Thus, the reproductive paths of full-blood and half-breed coyotes do not cross often enough to be a threat to the coyote.

Setting Up Housekeeping

In late January and into February, a female coyote in estrous attracts males from the surrounding countryside. They may stay with her for weeks vying for breeding rights. Eventually the female chooses one suitor, and the rest wander off. The pair travels and hunts together and may engage in a kind of courtship dance in which each rises on its hind legs and touches the other's forepaws with its own. The pair breeds, then sets out to locate a suitable place to whelp the pups.

The rest of the year may be spent above ground as an itinerant, but coyotes give birth to their young in the protection of an underground burrow. Often, the former home of a badger or skunk will be appropriated, although coyotes will dig their own burrows if necessary. Sometimes, coyote parents-to-be will prepare several dens, the extras to be used in the event that humans or other enemies discover the first one.

About two months after breeding, the female gives birth to a litter of hairless, helpless, blind pups, numbering from two to twelve (five or six is average). Each weighs about half a pound and is totally dependent on its parents. Except for nursing, the male coyote shares equally in pup rearing chores, which often means bringing food to the den for his lactating mate.

At about two weeks of age, the pups' teeth begin to appear, and the parents start to supplement their youngsters' milk diet with partially digested adult fare that is regurgitated at the burrow. In another month, the pups may be ready for tidbits of prey that have not seen the inside of their parents' stomachs.

Gradually, the pups learn the basic hunting skills by stalking grasshoppers and other insects near the den. They also spend a lot of time tumbling, wrestling, and establishing a pecking order among themselves. By mid-summer, the young-

Female coyote with pups at den, western Montana

sters are old enough to allow abandonment of the den, and the family assumes a seminomadic lifestyle. Many so-called coyote packs probably are traveling family units, although unrelated adults do sometimes hunt together, too. By late fall (if not before), the fully grown pups leave the family unit to seek their own niche in the coyote world.

Unpaired, adult coyotes can exhibit a variety of attitudes toward others of their kind, ranging from extreme antisocial behavior to the creation of loose kinships. Often, one coyote's tolerance of others is in direct proportion to the abundance of food nearby. Coyotes do not, however, form the highly structured packs typical of wolves. More often than not, the coyote is a loner, although mated pairs frequently stay together until death.

Coyotes maintain home ranges that vary in size from less than a single square mile to several dozen square miles. Typically, home ranges are smaller in the wooded terrain of the East than on the western prairies. Compared to other predators, such as wolves and cougars, coyotes are not very protective of the territory they inhabit. While groups of coyotes sometimes raise a ruckus when intruders enter their domain, singles and pairs usually do not defend established boundaries.

A coyote leaps over a small creek, Yellowstone National Park

Curiously, when conflicts do arise, coyotes almost never fight with members of the opposite sex.

Most coyotes do, however, let their presence be known by urinating or depositing scent from an anal gland on numerous rocks, bushes, and logs. When part of a kill is cached as a meal for tomorrow, it too may get a dose of urine—perhaps as a warning that the food is already spoken for. Researchers guess that every coyote can identify every other coyote by the smells they leave behind.

Coyotes also communicate vocally; in fact, they are considered to be the most vocal of all North American wildlife species. Naturalist Stanley Young described the most common coyote call as a "high, quavering staccato yip yap that often ends in a series of high, shrill-toned, ear-piercing howls." It is, he said, as if the coyote let out a prolonged howl, then ran after it and bit it into small pieces.

Early observers guessed that a mournful howl might be telling of pain, approaching bad weather, or even the death of another coyote. Modern researchers have identified at least nine different coyote vocalizations, including a huff, growl, woof, bark, whine, lone howl, and group yip-howl. Exactly what all these mean is still largely a mystery. The coyote's penchant for making noise is so universal, though, that some researchers are now using vocalizations to estimate local coyote populations. Coyote counters split the night air with taped coyote howls (or even an electronic siren), then record the number of coyote responses.

There's even a report (undocumented and possibly charged with imagination, but interesting nonetheless) of a coyote using its voice to foil a human pursuer. In *The Voice of the Coyote,* Frank Dobie relates the tale of a hunter on horseback who chased a coyote into tall grass. Galloping to the spot at which the coyote had last been seen, the man peered in every direction, but could see no sign of the predator. Then he heard the muffled, hollow barking of a coyote that sounded as though it were a long way off. Unable to believe that his quarry had gotten so far away (and perplexed that it would be barking at all), the hunter continued to search the nearby grass, and he soon discovered the coyote sneaking along on its belly. He surmised that the coyote had attempted to outwit him by barking into a badger hole.

Getting Along with Humankind

Outwitting—or at least adapting to—humans has long been the coyote's stock in trade. More than anything else, it is this ability that has prevented the coyote from going the way of the wolf, grizzly, and cougar.

Nowhere is this unique adaptive skill more evident than in the scattered populations of coyotes that have chosen to live within the boundaries of some of the continent's largest cities. In Los Angeles, for example, a few thousand coyotes den in culverts, raid gardens and garbage cans, get their drinks from lawn sprinklers or swimming pools, and eat dogfood (and sometimes the dog) from back porches.

In Lincoln, Nebraska (population 175,000), a male coyote established a variety of relationships with a dozen different dogs. Some he nipped on the rump, while others sent him packing. A female golden retriever held particular interest for the coyote, and the two spent a lot of time romping and chasing as though they were litter mates. The dog's owner put an end to the friendship, however, when the pair attempted to mate.

Some human residents are pleased to have coyotes at their back doors, although their food handouts do the animals a disservice by conditioning them to associate humans with food. Coyotes that lose all fear of humans can be dangerous. In 1982, a three-year-old girl was killed by a coyote while the youngster sat on a curb near her home in Glendale, California. While some human residents have called for the elimination of the coyote "menace," there's probably little city fathers could do even if they wanted to. Urban coyotes are likely here to stay.

Throughout the animal's range, humans continue to be the leading cause of death among coyotes. The animal's long-haired pelt brings top dollar at fur auctions, making it a popular target for trappers and sport hunters. Other coyotes starve during hard winters; wolves and cougars kill some; and mange, distemper, and internal parasites account for others. In captivity, coyotes have been known to live nearly twenty years, but in the wild average life expectancy probably does not exceed four years.

The coyote is one predator, though, that has little to worry about. With an expanded range and an overall population that is probably at an all-time peak, the coyote's future seems secure. And that is good. Most human residents of coyote country (some ranchers and misinformed deer hunters notably excluded) would certainly count it a loss should the coyote's howl no longer pierce the North American night. Perhaps naturalist Ernest T. Seton said it best: "If the day should ever come when one may camp and hear not a note of the coyote's joyous stirring evening song, I hope that I shall long before have passed away, gone over the Great Divide."

Foxes

They are the most ubiquitous of all the wild canines. In every U. S. state and Canadian province, they ply the trade of small carnivores—feeding on rodents, wild birds, and occasionally a farmer's chicken. Some have learned like the coyote to prosper from human presence. Others have suffered at the hands of man. Some are bold and open, while others remain secretive and all but invisible.

Perhaps more than any other animal, foxes have worked their way into our lexicon, with the reference usually concerning the creature's supposed cleverness. A particularly sneaky individual is "sly as a fox." One person who tricks another is said to have "outfoxed" his opponent. Devious people may also be as "crafty," "cunning," or "clever" as a fox.

In fiction, too, the fox has usually been a somewhat unsavory character, forever running off with a farmyard goose or pestering fluffy cottontail rabbits. It was, of course, a folklore fox that first rationalized a failure with the term "sour grapes." It's as if the fox personifies all the slightly negative qualities that people reluctantly admire.

In reality, of course, the foxes—there are four species (or five, depending upon who's doing the counting) in North America—are neither evil nor good. They are just small wild dogs trying to eke out a living from the woods, plains, and icepacks they inhabit.

Big Red

When most people think of a fox, the image that springs to mind is one of a large, red, bushy-tailed creature fleeing before hounds. This is the red fox, the most wide-ranging wild canine on the conti-

Red fox, western Montana

the tags earned a generous reward. Years later, it became apparent that the fox had little or nothing to do with the pheasant decline. Almost certainly, the real culprits were changing agricultural practices and loss of pheasant habitat.

Now that wolves have disappeared from most of North America, foxes have only one significant enemy—humans. The vagaries of the fur market often dictate the extent to which the animals are hunted and trapped, although reds are popular quarry any time. That they still exist in large numbers and in close proximity to humans is solid testimony to their tenacity and adaptive nature.

But the characteristic most often attributed to the red fox is cleverness. One story that is told again and again concerns the fox ridding itself of fleas, a plague common to many creatures who spend time in burrows. Supposedly, the fox takes in its mouth a piece of bark, ball of wool, stick, or similar tool and slowly backs into a lake or stream. Gradually, it sinks lower and lower into the water until only its nose and mouth are not submerged. The fleas, of course, have migrated to higher ground and now sit clustered on the bark, wool, or stick. The fox then lets go of the flea-laden tool and swims flealessly ashore. Various people, as far

back as the sixteenth century, claim to have witnessed this tonsorial feat.

Another testimonial to foxy ingenuity appeared in an Iowa newspaper around the turn of the century: A gentleman farmer happened to be watching a flock of ducks feeding in the shallow water at the end of a lake when a fox chanced upon the scene. After studying the situation, the fox (unseen by the ducks) traveled to the far end of the lake and set afloat several bunches of dead grass. These traveled with the current to the ducks, which showed no alarm at their arrival. Noting the ducks' acceptance of the floating grass, the fox took a huge bunch of grass in its jaws and slipped into the water. In a few moments, the predator had drifted and swum into the flock, at which point it grabbed a fat mallard and headed for shore to enjoy its meal.

Make of these tales what you will, but remember that wild animals are what they are and do only what their genes, instincts, and parental training allow them to do. Terms like "clever" and "dull" are human interpretations and have no real value in studying nature. Suffice it to say that the red fox is a capable predator that thrives both because of and in spite of humankind.

Red fox scratching

The Fox
That Climbs Trees

When Europeans first set foot in North America, life was difficult and recreational joys few. After a time, however, the thoughts of some immigrants turned to the sporting pleasures they had enjoyed in Europe, including fox hunting. Now fox hunting in Europe was (and continues to be) focused on the chase. The baying of hounds in pursuit of a fox rings like music in the ears of European sportsmen, and if the chase lasts all day, so much the better.

So, the new Americans set off with dogs and muskets to hunt the small, gray fox they occasionally saw in the woods and meadows of the virgin land. It took no time at all, however, for them to discover that this animal made a despicably unsporting quarry. Again and again, the hounds led them to the mouth of an underground burrow into which the gray fox had escaped. While the foxes they had known in Europe (red foxes) might run all day before a pack of dogs, the gray fox usually headed for a burrow at the first sign of trouble.

As if that were not bad enough, the gray fox had another frightful quality: it climbed trees. Frequently, the hunters had the disturbing experience of pursuing a gray fox right into the branches of a tree. It seemed totally unfoxlike, but there the animal was, a dozen or more feet off the ground looking down on them like a common housecat. It didn't take long for the immigrants to abandon fox hunting until they could import red foxes that would act as foxes should.

The gray fox is the only wild dog to climb trees, and for a long time most observers swore that it did so only when the tree tilted far toward the horizontal. Subsequent sightings have proven, however, that the gray fox can climb most vertical trunks quite easily. It does so with claws that are significantly longer, sharper, and more curved than those of the red fox. The gray may either bound up a tree like a cat or inch its way up by hugging the trunk like a bear.

Once in the tree's branches, the animal is fairly mobile, though it lacks the impressive arboreal agility of a squirrel or cat. Departing the tree may be accomplished with either the head or feet traveling first. Grays apparently feel quite at home in a tree and will use hollow trunks as dens in which to whelp their pups. One was even sighted in a vacant hawk nest, but it's unlikely that the nest was used for rearing young foxes.

Except for tree climbing, the gray and red fox are quite similar, and it is perhaps easiest to describe the gray by comparing the animal to its cousin. Tipping the scales at about eight pounds, the gray fox is a bit smaller than the red, and slightly shorter legs make it appear even more diminutive. It sports a speckled gray upper body and buff belly. Parts of its legs, tail, neck, and back are reddish orange. Black markings distinguish its nose, muzzle, and head.

The gray is a very secretive creature, even more nocturnal than the red fox. It is possible for the animal to keep its presence secret from all but the most observant humans. With the exception of some plains states and the Rocky Mountains, the gray fox exists border to border and coast to coast in the United States. Though once numerous in parts of Canada, it virtually disappeared there for a time, but has recently reestablished itself in three places near the U. S. border. It also thrives throughout Central America.

The gray can get by in a variety of habitats, but seems to prefer broken, hilly, rocky terrain with plenty of brush and cover. One definite requirement seems to be the nearby presence of trees, which probably accounts for its absence from the plains states. It gets along well near cities, and garbage dumps often become favored scavenging grounds.

In diet, reproduction, and many other behaviors, the gray is quite similar to the red fox. It has been known to eat virtually every kind of meat, fruit, vegetable, or insect, although small mammals are the preferred fare. About four pups are born in late spring, and by winter they are independent. Hunting technique is much like that of the red fox, although the gray typically covers only a small portion of its home range on any given night and relies heavily on vision to locate prey.

Unlike its red relative, the gray may do much of its sleeping in a den, even when no pups are being reared. It also lacks the extreme wariness of the red fox. Grays are easy marks for even the most novice trapper, but its coarse fur is not highly valued, so trapping and hunting pressures are usually light. Besides humans, the only creatures to prey on gray foxes are an occasional bobcat, coyote, or eagle.

Perhaps naturalist Ernest T. Seton described the gray fox best: "If we mix equal parts of red fox, coon, and bobcat, and season the combination with a strong dash of cottontail rabbit, we shall have the gray fox's disposition synthetically produced," he wrote. "The gray fox is less swift, less strong, and less cunning than its cousin, the red fox. The one is a bandit, the other a burglar."

Outfoxing the Cold

There lives on the frozen tundra of the far north the most unique of America's wild canines—the arctic fox. Perfectly adapted for life in a winter wasteland, this diminutive creature thrives where few other animals can even exist. Engaged in a perpetual battle of survival against the elements, this snowland scavenger and hunter repeatedly emerges victorious.

The arctic fox weighs only seven pounds and stands barely a foot high at the shoulder. Its thick coat belies the fact that this fox is smaller than many housecats. The snowshoe hares that populate the north in cyclical abundance often have little to fear from this tiny predator—not because the fox cannot catch them, but because it likely could not defeat the ten-pound hare in a fight.

Arctic foxes are holarctic, meaning they inhabit the tundra of North America, Europe, Asia, Greenland, and Iceland. Only food shortages can compel them to venture south of treeline.

The fox of the north exists in two distinct, genetically determined color phases. Dark phase animals, which occur mostly in coastal areas, vary from blue-black to gray, depending on the season. The inland dwellers, the white phase, are pure white in winter and brown, gray, or yellow in the summer. Most of the arctic foxes in Alaska and Canada are of the white phase.

Both types of foxes are highly valued for their thick and beautiful fur. Their curious nature and acceptance of man make them easy targets for trappers, and each year tens of thousands are captured. For many decades, fur from the tiny arctic fox has provided most—if not all—of the cash income for many Eskimo families. However, as economic development brings new types of employment to the North, the number of trappers dwindles. Fox populations do follow a boom and bust cycle, but it is probably more closely tied to lemming numbers than to fur prices. For now, the little fox is doing just fine.

What the arctic fox lacks in size, it makes up for in tenacity and toughness. When winter storms sweep snow across the land, most of the fox's warm-weather food supplies disappear. Lemmings and other rodents either hibernate or vanish beneath the snow. Most birds head south. Vegetation shrivels and dies. It is then that the arctic fox shows its mettle.

Some head inland to follow the caribou herds, hoping to steal a meal from a wolf kill. Others turn to the vast expanse of pack ice, where they become scavengers, using their keen sense of smell to locate the remains of dead creatures. No one knows for sure just what the icepack foxes do eat, but sea birds, algae, invertebrates, and fish are likely part of the bill of fare. It's suspected that a fox can go two weeks without food, and enough carrion apparently exists to meet this meager need. Some probably do die of starvation, however.

Red fox pups resting near den site

The foxes also get their share of meat from sea mammals (mostly seals and walruses) by adopting a polar bear as a meal ticket. As the bruin lumbers across the ice, the fox follows close behind. The quicker fox has nothing to fear from the bear as long as it does not get too close. When the bear kills a seal, walrus, or other large prey, there are invariably plenty of scraps left for the fox to eat. The bear does not appear to get anything out of the deal.

Occasionally, a sojourning fox may experience the treat of stumbling upon a walrus carcass that has not already been devoured by polar bears. If no competition shows up, this could provide an entire winter's provender. More likely, however, other foxes will arrive to share the feast. Researchers once discovered forty foxes feeding on one walrus carcass frozen into the sea ice off Alaska. The scavengers had hacked their way through a foot and a half of ice, chewed a large hole in the tough walrus hide, and were feasting inside, oblivious to the raging winter.

Winter travel by arctic foxes is nothing short of phenomenal. They have been spotted 400 miles north of the Alaskan coast and within twenty-five miles of the north pole. One fox was trapped

Arctic fox

1,200 miles from where it had been tagged by scientists, and another animal trapped in Alaska carried a Russian tag.

Several factors contribute to fox survival in the face of the toughest conditions nature has to offer. They sport a coat of thick, luxuriant fur that traps a large amount of insulating air between hairs. Even the soles of their feet are covered with hair. Their small size offers little resistance to the harsh winds, and—like other northern animals—the foxes are adept at exposing as little of themselves as possible to the elements. Small ears and short legs help in this regard. The foxes also know that when the temperature dips to about minus 60° F, it's time to retreat into a temporary snow den. They can apparently increase their metabolism to produce more heat. One guess is that the arctic fox can survive temperatures as low as minus 95° F.

But even the great northland is not an icebox year-round. In early spring, the normally solitary foxes begin their return to the mainland, where they will mate and give birth to their young before the abundant food supply of summer arrives. Arctic foxes are the most prolific North American canine, producing as many as twenty-five pups in a single litter (ten or fifteen might be average, however). This high reproductive rate is testimony to the fact that most young never make it to adulthood in the harsh North.

On riverbanks or on ridges high above the ocean's shoreline, a mated pair of foxes sets up housekeeping in the same den that has been used by others of their kind for many generations. Often, new tenants feel the need to improve upon past diggings, and many dens feature one hundred or more entrances. Over the years, droppings and food scraps accumulate around den sites and act as fertilizer to fuel plant growth. From above, it's easy to spot a fox den by the rich green foliage surrounding it. Popular denning areas—those in sandy soil on well-drained slopes above the permafrost—often become thoroughly dotted with telltale lush spots of green.

The young are born blind, helpless, and about the size of a mouse. For a fortnight or so after the birth of the pups, the male provides food for the entire family. In a few weeks, however, the youngsters are ready to accompany their parents on foraging trips, and—usually—the hunting is good. It is summer now, and the northland teems with life. Dark phase foxes (coastal dwellers) feast on ocean carrion that washes ashore. The inland white phase foxes raid bird nests (which are on the ground, of course, because there are no trees) for the eggs and the adults. Later in the season, berries become popular fox fare.

Lemmings are the favorite prey of arctic foxes, and a single fox family may consume as many as one hundred per day. Not surprisingly, fox num-

bers can rise and fall in response to the notoriously cyclic lemming population extremes. Foxes also feed upon ground squirrels, young hares, and birds that become flightless when they molt.

As a hedge against winter, arctic foxes have developed a caching ability more like that of a squirrel than a canine. When hunting is good, huge amounts of dead prey may be stockpiled for consumption during lean times. One scientist found forty-two birds (mostly young ones) and a large number of eggs in one cache, all laid out in neat rows. He estimated that the fox could have lived for a month off this larder. A dash of urine at a cache marks it with the signature of its owner, and it was once thought that no fox would raid the pantry of another. Recent observations, however, have proven that claim false.

Another peculiarity of the fox of the north is its almost nonexistent fear of man. Virtually every researcher or oil worker who has spent time in the Arctic returns with stories about the little fellow's brazenness. One camper turned away from his wash basin for a moment only to look back and see a fox escaping with his bar of soap in its mouth. The little thieves are also notorious for running off with all manner of tools.

Red fox searching for food in snow

In earlier days, explorers sometimes stabbed the inquisitive (and perhaps ravenous) foxes by accident when the predators got too close to seal-skinning operations. Today, the garbage generated by a scientific or oil exploration camp is likely to attract foxes from miles around. At one such place, the many foxes turned into downright pests, and an Eskimo trapper was brought in to reduce their numbers. He captured 200.

In 1741, a Russian explorer and his crew became shipwrecked on Bering Island. Healthy crew members first carried ashore several men suffering from scurvy and other diseases. Depositing them on the beach, the crew went back to the ship for others. When they returned with another load of victims, they found arctic foxes attacking the first group just as they might any large but weak prey that chanced to wash ashore.

Biologist Larry Underwood tells of the time he bent to listen intently at an arctic fox den that might contain pups. Suddenly something tugged at his hair. Turning around, he found himself nose to nose with an adult fox that apparently did not want any visitors at her den. Underwood jumped up and yelled, but the fox gave not an inch. As it snapped and barked like a watchdog, the little fox

Kit fox pups playing near den

forced Underwood into retreat. This canine is indeed in control of the northland.

Kit and Swift Foxes

Two more wild canines—the kit fox and the swift fox—hunt the ravines and roadsides of North America. They are remarkably alike, and biologists have trouble deciding whether the pair should be separated into two species or lumped together in one.

The physical differences are slight at best: the size of the ears, distance between them, length of the tail, and shading of coat color. More diagnostic might be the territory each inhabits, the swift preferring the northern prairies and the kit the desert biome of the Southwest. A lay observer lucky enough to spot one of these creatures might do well to look at his map rather than at the fox in attempting to determine its pedigree. The rest of this section will treat them as one animal (arbitrarily called the kit fox).

The kit is the smallest of all the wild American canines, tipping the scales at a mere five pounds. Even the lowly jackrabbit might prove to be a formidable adversary. The kit sports a gray or tan coat with a darker back and a buff throat and belly. The tail is tipped with black, and either side of the muzzle carries a splash of the same color. Often, the most noticeable characteristic is its ears, which seem disproportionately large. Perhaps the adjective most often used to describe the little fox is "delicate." Because of its diminutive size, the kit seems to fairly float across the prairie on those occasions when it hits its top speed of twenty-five mph.

Once common in the West and Midwest, the kit fox became an innocent victim of the war between ranchers and large predators. Very much a scavenger, the kit was not shy about visiting the poison bait stations set out to kill wolves and coyotes. Also, the animals seem to be quite unafraid of humans, making them relatively easy targets for trap and gun. In just a few decades, kit populations plummeted. Today, the kit fox inhabits parts of most states west of the Mississippi, but its numbers are thought to be extremely low.

It's difficult to be certain, however, because the kit fox is quiet, shy, and almost totally nocturnal. At sunset the predator emerges from its den, lounges in the area for a short time, then goes on the hunt. The night is spent meandering through its home range, and the first rays of dawn find the fox again at its den site. Kit foxes are so secretive that they often share their habitat with people without the latter ever knowing they're there.

Kits are more closely tied to their dens than any other foxes. One of the subterranean homes might extend for thirty feet through sandy soil and have numerous entrances. Tunnel diameter might be only seven to ten inches, testimony to the kit's small size. Dens are often found in barren, overgrazed pastures that provide virtually no cover for the animal.

The kit fox's diet includes such delicacies as ground squirrels, mice, baby rabbits, and a host of other prey ranging from small birds to insects. A researcher once examined five kit stomachs and discovered them to be packed full of army worms that the foxes apparently had found appetizing. The kit has learned to make good use of road-killed prey; in fact, many of the infrequent kit sightings by humans are made from a passing car. Kits also appear to frequent highway areas for the warmth that emanates from the pavement. Consequently, many of the little foxes are killed by cars. Human hunters, coyotes, and eagles also take kit lives.

Kits usually breed in mid-winter and give birth to about four pups in March or April. They were once thought to be monogamous, but this is not the case. By the time they're three months old, the pups are nearly as large as their parents, but the family continues to hunt together until fall.

Poisons (many of which are now illegal) are no longer a major problem for the foxes, and there are some indications that kit numbers are on the rise. Habitat loss continues to be a problem, however, and it's unlikely that the kit fox will ever become as ubiquitous as it was before westward expansion.

Afterword

So it is that humans, to a great extent, control the future of America's wild dogs. We have the power to let them live and the tools to wipe them out. Now let us pray that we also will have the wisdom to treat them as fellow travelers, not adversaries. Let us hope that we can put away our poisons and our hatred and commit ourselves once and for all to a future of living in harmony with the wolves, coyotes, foxes, and other creatures with whom we share this Earth.

Perhaps we need to look back to our earliest ancestors, the primitive men and women who first beckoned the wolf in from the cold. They knew, I think, what we have forgotten—that humans and animals are all part of the same natural world. That in nature there is no such thing as good and evil. And, most important, that there is really room here for all of us.

For Further Reading

The Wolf

Brown, David.
Wolf in the Southwest: The Making of an Endangered Species. Tucson: University of Arizona Press, 1983.

Fox, Michael.
Soul of the Wolf. Boston: Little, Brown and Co., 1980.

Fox, Michael.
The Wild Canids: Their Systematics, Behavioral Ecology & Evolution. 1975. Reprint. Melbourne, Florida: R. E. Krieger, 1984.

Lopez, Barry.
Of Wolves and Men. New York: Charles Scribner's Sons, 1979.

Mech, L. David.
The Wolf: The Ecology and Behavior of an Endangered Species. Minneapolis: University of Minnesota Press, 1981.

Young, Stanley, and Edward Goldman.
The Wolves of North America. Dover Publications, 1944.

The Coyote

Cadieux, Charles L.
Coyotes: Predators & Survivors. Washington, D. C.: Stone Wall Press, 1983.

Dobie, Frank.
The Voice of the Coyote. Lincoln: University of Nebraska Press, 1961.

Leydet, Francois.
The Coyote: Defiant Songdog of the West. Norman: University of Oklahoma Press, 1981.

Pringle, Laurence.
The Controversial Coyote. San Diego: Harcourt, Brace, Jovanovich, Inc., 1977.

Ryden, Hope.
God's Dog. New York: Viking Penquin, Inc., 1979.

Young, Stanley, and Hartley H. Jackson.
The Clever Coyote. Lincoln: University of Nebraska Press, 1978.

The Fox

Rue, Leonard Lee.
The World of the Red Fox. Philadelphia: J. B. Lippincott Co., 1969.

GARY TURBAK, a native of South Dakota, is a full-time freelance writer whose work has appeared in *Equinox, Reader's Digest, Field and Stream, National* and *International Wildlife, Writer's Digest,* and many other widely circulated periodicals. In addition, he has published four non-fiction books. On a more personal note, he is a Vietnam veteran, a cat lover, a former teacher, a professional photographer, and a lifelong student of wildlife. Turbak and his wife live in Missoula, Montana.

ALAN CAREY is a professional wildlife photographer whose work has appeared in such publications as *National Wildlife, Smithsonian,* and *National Geographic World.* His love of wildlife and his desire to photograph America's animals and birds in their natural habitats have taken him from the Florida Everglades to the frozen Alaskan tundra.